Constructive Dismissal

By Daniel Barnett

The Employment Law Library

All books in the Employment Law Library are sent for free to members of the HR Inner Circle.

1. Employee Investigations

2. GDPR for HR Professionals

3. Preventing and Defending Employee Stress Claims

4. Employment Tribunal Time Limits

5. Deconstructing TUPE

6. Changing Terms & Conditions

7. Constructive Dismissal

Forthcoming:
Grievances

Published by Employment Law Services Limited, Unit 3, Chequers Farm, Chequers Lane, Watford, Hertfordshire WD25 0LG

ISBN 978-1-913925-00-0

Acknowledgments

This is the seventh in my series of small employment law books. They are designed to give HR Professionals a solid grounding in a subject which you won't learn about through normal avenues. The content is at a similar level to undergraduate LLB degree courses, so anyone who is familiar with this book will know as much any junior lawyer.

I'd like to thank Victoria Gough for her help with the content, Eugenie Verney for proofreading, Jennie Hargrove for editing and Tincuta Moscaliuc for her – as always – fantastic work on cover design and internal layout.

Daniel Barnett
September 2020

ABOUT THE AUTHOR

 Daniel Barnett is a leading employment law barrister practising from Outer Temple Chambers. With 25 years' experience defending public and private sector employers against employment claims, he has represented a Royal Family, several international airlines, FTSE-100 companies and various NHS Trusts and local authorities. Employee clients include David & Victoria Beckham's nanny and Paul Mason (subject of the ITV documentary 'Britain's Fattest Man').

Daniel is a past chair of the Employment Lawyers' Association's publishing committee and electronic services working party. He is the author or co-author of eight books, including the Law Society Handbook on Employment Law (currently in its 8th edition). He is the creator of the Employment Law (UK) mailing list, an email alerter bulletin service sending details of breaking news in employment law three times a week to 30,000 recipients.

Legal directories describe him as 'extremely knowledgeable and [he] can absorb pages of instructions at lightning speed', 'involved in a number of highly contentious matters', 'singled out for his work for large blue-chip companies', 'combination of in-depth legal knowledge, pragmatism, quick response times and approachability', 'inexhaustible', 'tenacious', 'knowledgeable', and 'an excellent advocate'.

He is one of the leading speakers and trainers on the employment law and HR circuit. He has presented seminars for the House of Commons, the BBC, Oxford University, HSBC, Barclays Bank, Ocado, and dozens of other organisations in-house. In 2013, 2014, 2016, and 2019 he designed — and was the sole speaker at — the Employment Law MasterClass national tour.

As well as full-time practice as a barrister and speaker, Daniel is the founder of the HR Inner Circle – a membership club for smart, ambitious HR Professionals. In 2007, he co-founded CPD Webinars Ltd, then the UK's leading webinar training company for lawyers, and sold it to Thomson Reuters in 2011.

Daniel is widely sought after as a commentator in both broadcast and print media on all legal issues. Since 2010 he has presented the Legal Hour on LBC Radio. In 2019, he launched Employment Law Matters, a weekly podcast with short explanations of employment law topics. Subscribe at www.danielbarnett.co.uk/podcast

www.danielbarnett.co.uk
Outer Temple Chambers
Strand, London

Contents

THESE BONUS RESOURCES ARE AVAILABLE IN THE VAULT TO ALL PURCHASERS OF GETTING REDUNDANCY RIGHT:

One complimentary place at Daniel Barnett's next 'HR Secrets' seminar tour (the previous tour took place in 15 cities around the UK, with topics including holiday pay, spotting malingering, and top mistakes made by HR Professionals)
FIRST 100 PURCHASERS ONLY | Value: £120

Daniel Barnett's template redundancy selection matrix, which you can use to score employees during a selection process
Value: £75

Daniel Barnett's redundancy policy, which he uses with his regular corporate clients
Value: £100

Private online forum, where you can discuss issues arising from redundancies and ask questions
Value: £125

3 x live Zoom Q&A sessions with expert guest speakers on redundancy
Value: £100

Access to videos of 31 webinars chaired by Daniel Barnett in early 2020, with 31 employment barristers on 31 aspects of employment law
Value: £60

Part 1
Overview

1. Introduction

Constructive dismissal is a term which is often misused and misunderstood. It is a specific legal claim which the employee can bring if the employer's conduct has seriously breached the employee's contract of employment. This serious breach of contract entitles the employee to resign and say they were dismissed.

It can be tempting to be a bit flippant about constructive dismissals. Such claims are notoriously difficult for employees to win but defending them can be time consuming and costly. It isn't enough to know where to find the legal definition and understand it. Employers need to know how to spot the kind of incident and behaviour that leads to these claims being brought.

The legal concept is complex and multi-faceted. What sort of a breach will be serious enough? What must the employee do in response to preserve a tribunal claim? And, perhaps most importantly, how can employers avoid these claims?

Starting point: the employment contract

The employment contract is the collection of terms and conditions that the parties have agreed will govern the employment relationship. These days most contracts are written documents, but verbal agreements can also be binding. The cornerstone of a constructive dismissal claim is the serious breach of contract by the employer, often called a 'fundamental' or 'repudiatory' breach. The theory is that an employee can treat the contract as if it has ended if the employer seriously breaches it. The employee can then take steps to act on that breach by resigning. The resignation brings the contract to a formal end (the 'dismissal' bit) but it is the employer's repudiatory breach that prompts it (the 'constructive' bit).

The legal definition

Section 95(1)(c) of the *Employment Rights Act 1996* sets out the legal definition of constructive dismissal:

'...an employee is dismissed by his employer if...the employee terminates the contract under which he is employed (with or without notice) in circumstances in which he is entitled to terminate it without notice by reason of the employer's conduct'.

There are three key elements here:

1. The employer's conduct — the significant or 'repudiatory' breach of contract. This breach must be so serious that it goes to the root of the contract or shows that the employer doesn't intend to be bound by its terms anymore.

2. The employee's entitlement to resign without notice because of the breach (even if the employee gives notice).

3. The employee's action — the resignation in response to that breach. Conversely, the employee may choose to do nothing, and 'waive' (ignore and accept) the breach, which means the contract continues and there is no dismissal, constructive or otherwise. An employee must not delay too long before resigning in response to the breach or they may inadvertently waive the breach.

We will look at each of these elements in detail throughout this book.

Is a constructive dismissal always unfair?

If an employee is constructively dismissed, they will usually have a claim for notice pay unless they have worked or been paid their notice already. This notice pay claim is called a wrongful dismissal claim (another term which is often misused). The notice pay claim arises because the constructive dismissal — the breach of contract which entitles the employee to resign without notice — has denied the employee of their notice period and pay.

An unfair dismissal claim is different. If an employee is constructively dismissed, they still need two years' continuous service to bring an unfair dismissal claim. If an employee has less than two years' service, then they can't normally bring a claim for constructive unfair dismissal.

Technically, a constructive dismissal could be fair because the same legal test of fairness applies to a constructive dismissal as any dismissal. The statutory test of fairness is set out in section 98(4) of the *Employment Rights Act 1996*. This section says that the question of whether a dismissal is fair or unfair depends on whether the employer acted reasonably in treating the reason for dismissal as sufficient reason for dismissing the employee.

What is 'reasonable' will depend on the size of the employer and the administrative resources available to it (bigger employers will have more resources and might be expected to jump through greater administrative hoops before dismissing an employee). It is an objective test and a tribunal must decide whether the decision to dismiss fell within the range of reasonable responses that a reasonable employer might have adopted.

There is nothing in law to say a constructive dismissal is always unfair. As in any unfair dismissal case, an employment tribunal must look at the employer's conduct and decide whether its actions were reasonable. Nevertheless, it will almost always be impossible for an employer to show that it acted reasonably in seriously breaching the employee's contract. Fair constructive dismissals are extremely rare. In *Welch v The Taxi Owners Association (UKEATS/0001/12/BI)*, the employer unilaterally reduced the employee's hours of work due to a downturn in business. The employee resigned. The Employment Appeal Tribunal agreed there had been a fundamental breach of contract — the unilateral reduction in hours — but said there was no unfair dismissal because there were legitimate business reasons to reduce the employee's hours. Employers shouldn't rely on this decision, though, as unilateral variation always carries risks.

Remember that there may be other kinds of claims that the employee could bring based on poor treatment, such as discrimination. Just because an employee doesn't have the continuous service to bring a constructive dismissal claim doesn't necessarily mean the employer is in the clear.

2.   Repudiatory breach: what kind of term must be breached?

In order to bring a claim for constructive dismissal, an employee will have to identify a repudiatory breach of contract. The breach can be of an express term or an implied term. It can be an actual breach of contract that has happened already, or something the employer is planning to do in future (an 'anticipatory' breach). It can be a one-off act or a series of acts or incidents which together create a repudiatory breach. Let's look at each of these things in turn.

Express and implied terms

Express terms are the ones that are expressly agreed between the parties, whether verbally or in writing. An employment contract will set out what the employer agrees to pay the employee in return for the work they have agreed to do. If the employee does the work and the employer fails to pay the employee as agreed in the contract, that is a breach of an express term. The concept of payment in return for work is a fundamental part of the contract of employment, so failing to pay will be a fundamental breach of it. It could give rise to a constructive dismissal claim if the employee resigns in response.

A constructive dismissal can also arise from the breach of an implied term of the contract. An implied term is something that is implied into a contract to make it work. For example, if an employment contract for an HGV driver does not stipulate the requirement for an HGV driving licence, that requirement will be implied into the contract between the driver and the company. Terms can also be implied by custom and practice, such as a change in hours of work that might develop over time and differ from the written terms given at the start of the employment relationship. The most common implied term that is relevant to constructive dismissal is the implied relationship of trust and confidence between employer and employee. If the employer behaves in a way which fundamentally breaches this implied term, the employee can resign and claim constructive dismissal. The breach of this implied term forms the basis of many constructive dismissal claims, and we will be looking at this in more detail in Part 2.

Must the breach have occurred already?

It is possible for something that hasn't yet happened to form the basis of a constructive dismissal claim. If an employer does something to show that it doesn't intend to be bound by contractual terms, that can be an anticipatory breach of contract. If an employer indicates that they intend to unilaterally demote the employee in a way that is not allowed by the contract, that is an anticipatory breach of contract. The employee is entitled to resign before the demotion takes effect and claim constructive dismissal. This happened in *Norwest Holst Group v Harrison [1985] IRLR 240*. The employee was a director at the employer's Derby office. He was told that the Derby office was closing at the end of the month. He was required to move to the Chesterfield office, but his director role would end. The employee resigned before the end of the month and claimed constructive dismissal. The Court of Appeal agreed that the employer's actions fundamentally breached the employee's contract even before the move took effect (though in this case the employee ultimately lost his constructive dismissal claim because he had delayed in accepting the breach).

What about if the employer gives notice that some change will be imposed unless the employee agrees to it — can that be an anticipatory breach of contract? There is some contradictory case law in this area, but the overwhelming view is that giving lawful notice cannot be an anticipatory breach of contract. In *Kerry Foods v Lynch [2005] IRLR 680*, the employee worked Monday to Friday as an area sales manager. Other managers also worked Saturdays. The employer asked the employee if he would agree to work Saturdays, but he refused. The employer sent him a letter giving him notice that his current contract would terminate at the end of his notice period if he did not agree to work Saturdays. The letter said he would be offered immediate re-engagement on a six-day-a-week contract. An employment tribunal found that this proposed change damaged the relationship of trust and confidence so seriously that it was a repudiatory breach. The employee had been constructively dismissed. The EAT disagreed, saying that giving notice lawfully and offering immediate re-engagement was not a repudiatory breach of contract.

Employers must remember that giving notice will always create a dismissal from the original contract, even if the employee is immediately reengaged on a new one. This dismissal might in some cases be unfair. Conduct which leads up to giving an employee lawful notice can also constitute a serious breach of contract. Employers should be cautious when changing terms and conditions. If an employer behaves in an aggressive or overbearing way in relation to changing terms and conditions, their behaviour in seeking to impose changes might be a repudiatory breach of the implied term of trust and confidence, even if the threat to serve notice is not.

One-off acts and courses of conduct

The repudiatory breach in a constructive dismissal claim can come from a single act, such as demoting an employee or failing to pay them. More often though, constructive dismissal claims are based on alleged poor treatment over a period of time. Claim forms often run to many pages involving numerous alleged incidents, protagonists, and witnesses. Defending a claim can be messy and time consuming, with evidence running to numerous lever arch files. It can be tough seeing the wood for the trees, with lots of irrelevant details to filter through before you get to the nub of the issue. Only by understanding how these claims are constructed can employers start to appreciate both how to defend them and how to avoid them occurring in the first place.

3. The last straw

When an employee resigns after a series of events, they usually claim that it was one final act which pushed them over the edge and made them resign. This last act is often referred to as the last straw. The whole series of events, taken together, can amount to a breach of the relationship of trust and confidence. Just as the final straw which breaks the camel's back isn't very heavy on its own, the last event may not be very serious. It doesn't have to be weighty enough to tip the balance on its own but needs to add something to the scales so that it contributes towards the balance tipping. The test is whether the action of the employer taken as a whole, over time, demonstrates that it didn't intend to be bound by the terms of the employment contract.

All employers will have dealt with this kind of complaint in some form or other, even if they haven't faced a constructive dismissal claim. Most employee grievances aren't about a single event and will refer to things which have happened over many months or years. There will always be one last event which tipped the balance and made them raise the grievance.

The last straw must add something

The last straw has to add something to the breach, however insignificant. A perfectly legitimate act by the employer can never be the last straw. In *Waltham Forest v Omilaju [2005] IRLR 35*, the employee brought various employment tribunal claims against the employer. The employer had a policy that employees who brought tribunal claims should apply for special leave or annual leave in order to attend their tribunal hearings. When the employer applied this policy and refused to pay the employee's salary while he attended the hearing, he resigned and said it was the last straw in a series of poor treatment episodes which had destroyed trust and confidence. The employee lost his original tribunal claims and issued a new one for constructive dismissal. The Court of Appeal said that the last straw must be the last in a series of incidents which, taken together, amount to a repudiatory breach of contract. They set the following guidelines about the last straw:

- The last straw must not be completely trivial

- It doesn't have to be the same character of incident as earlier ones in the series

- The last straw doesn't have to be unreasonable or blameworthy conduct on the part of the employer by itself, although in most cases it will be

- A completely harmless act by the employer cannot be the last straw even if the employee honestly but mistakenly thinks it undermines their trust and confidence in the employer.

The Court of Appeal did not agree that the employee had been constructively dismissed. The refusal to pay him for attending the tribunal, in line with its own policies, wasn't capable of being a last straw.

In the recent case of *Williams v Governing Body of Alderman Davies Church in Wales Primary School [2020] IRLR 589* however, the EAT held that if the last straw is entirely innocuous, that does not necessarily thwart a successful constructive dismissal claim. The previous poor conduct of the employer is relevant, where the breach has not been affirmed. HHJ Auerbach:

"so long as there has been conduct which amounts to a fundamental breach, [the breach has not been affirmed], and the employee does resign at least partly in response to it, constructive dismissal is made out. That is so, even if other, more recent, conduct has also contributed to the decision to resign."

While an innocuous act cannot be a last straw, it will not negate the effect of previous breaches, providing the breaches have not been affirmed.

Can a disciplinary process ever be the last straw?

Employers can get quite nervous about applying a disciplinary process to employees who are known to be difficult or serial complainers, fearful that whatever they do will come back to bite them. In some cases where there is a history of problems between an employer and employee, there may be things which happened in the past — repudiatory breaches — that the employee has waived by doing nothing and staying in employment (this is called affirmation and we will look at this more in Part 3). At some point later, the situation becomes too much for the employee and they resign in response to a last straw. The Court of Appeal has confirmed that an employee can rely on the whole course of conduct, including any previously waived repudiatory breaches, because the last straw 'revives' them. The case of *Kaur v Leeds Teaching Hospitals NHS Trust [2018] IRLR 833* also considered whether a fair disciplinary process — no matter what the outcome — can ever be that last straw.

Ms Kaur was a nurse. She had an altercation with a colleague. She was disciplined and given a final written warning for her inappropriate behaviour. She appealed against the warning but was unsuccessful. She resigned claiming constructive dismissal. Her claim was based on a series of events which, taken together, seriously breached trust and confidence. The events included alleged unjustified complaints about her performance, the altercation with her colleague, and the employer's conduct of the disciplinary process. She said that the employer's dismissal of her appeal against the final written warning was the last straw.

The employer applied to have the claim struck out because the employee had no chance of winning. The employment tribunal agreed she had no reasonable prospects of success and struck out the claim. The employee appealed and the case ended up in the Court of Appeal. The Court of Appeal reviewed and clarified the law on 'last straws' in constructive dismissal cases. Where there is a course of conduct which cumulatively creates a repudiatory breach of contract, the last act in that series can revive earlier affirmed breaches. If Ms Kaur had accepted earlier breaches by not resigning at that point, a new breach of contract could revive them. Theoretically she could bring a constructive dismissal claim. However, the Court of Appeal confirmed that a fair disciplinary process can never form part of a serious breach of contract. As a result, the appeal decision could not be a 'last straw'.

What sort of things can be a last straw?

It's impossible to give a definitive list of last straws because every case is different. I've given some examples below as a guide, including some from real cases:

- In cases where an employee has been bullied by her manager over time, a negative comment about a piece of work made in front of colleagues

- Another discriminatory act, even a minor one, in a series of discriminatory acts by an employer

- A decision made in a flawed or otherwise unfair grievance or disciplinary process, including appeals.

And what can't?

- A reasonable request to do work that falls within the employee's job description, remit and capabilities

- A solicitor's letter containing a 'without prejudice' offer of financial settlement in return for the employee's resignation (if correspondence is genuinely without prejudice it cannot be referred to in legal proceedings, as a last straw or anything else)

- The outcome of a fair and reasonable disciplinary or grievance process, including appeals.

Last word on the last straw

It can be easy to get wrapped up in mental knots when considering last straws and courses of conduct, but the overall message is a positive one for employers. Provided employers follow their own fair procedures, act in good faith and have reasonable grounds for making their decisions, whatever action they take is unlikely to constitute a 'last straw' that breaks the metaphorical camel's back. It's when fair and reasonable procedures aren't followed that an employer is more likely to come unstuck.

In Part 2 we will look in more detail at repudiatory breaches, including a detailed analysis of the implied duty of trust and confidence and how it comes into play in constructive dismissal cases.

Part 2
The Implied Term

In the first part of this book, we started looking at repudiatory breaches and what kind of act or behaviour can produce a serious breach of contract. Now we will take a deep dive into the implied term of mutual trust and confidence which often comes into play in constructive dismissal cases.

4. Implied term of mutual trust and confidence

The House of Lords set out the legal test for this kind of constructive dismissal in a case called *Malik v Bank of Credit and Commerce International [1997] IRLR 462*:

> '*The employer must not, without reasonable and proper cause, conduct itself in a manner calculated and likely to destroy or seriously damage the relationship of trust and confidence between employer and employee.*'

There are two things at play here: the employer's conduct and the potential 'reasonable and proper cause' for that conduct.

Does the employer's conduct have to be 'calculated'?

Malik suggests that the employer's conduct must be *calculated* to damage the relationship of trust and confidence **and** *likely* to do so (emphasis added). However, case law has confirmed that the test is an either/or test. The employer's conduct must *either* be calculated to destroy or seriously damage the employment relationship *or* be likely to do so. It doesn't have to be both.

The employer's intent is irrelevant if their behaviour is likely to damage the relationship. There doesn't need to be any kind of negative motive. If an employer's actions are likely to cause serious damage to the employment relationship then the term is breached, even if the act is an employer's honest mistake. The question a tribunal will ask is whether the employee could reasonably be expected to put up with the employer's conduct. It is an objective test. An employment tribunal will look at all the facts and come to a sensible judgment.

Motive might nonetheless be part of the overall picture

Although an employer doesn't need to intend to damage trust and confidence in order to breach the duty, their intention might be something that the tribunal considers as part of its objective assessment. In *Tullett Prebon v BGC Brokers [2011] IRLR 420*, some employees resigned to move to a competitor. They claimed they had been constructively dismissed, primarily to invalidate their post-termination restrictive covenants: if an employer has seriously breached the employment contract, they cannot rely on post-termination restrictions contained in the same contract. The High Court considered the employer's motive for certain acts which the employees said had breached trust and confidence. The Court of Appeal said the original court was right to consider the employer's motive. Although the employer's intention is irrelevant to the question of whether there has been a breach of trust and confidence (if their behaviour is likely to damage trust and confidence), their general intentions are relevant because they may show whether they intended to abandon or refuse to be bound by the terms of the employment contract.

Honest mistakes

The upshot is that an employer can make an honest mistake and still breach the implied term. In *Transco v O'Brien [2002] IRLR 444*, the employer offered new and more favourable contracts to all permanent employees for good commercial reasons. They didn't offer Mr O'Brien a new contract because they mistakenly thought that he wasn't a permanent employee (he had originally started the job through an agency). The Court of Appeal said that the employer's failure to offer the enhanced terms to the employee was a clear breach of the implied term of trust and confidence, even though it was based on a mistake. The fact that they didn't 'mean it' was irrelevant.

What does 'reasonable and proper cause' mean?

There is more to a breach of the implied term of trust and confidence than the employer destroying or seriously damaging trust and confidence (or behaving in a way that is calculated or likely to do so). The employee must also prove that the employer had no 'reasonable and proper cause' for their actions.

In *Hilton v Shiner [2001] IRLR 727*, the Employment Appeal Tribunal found that the demotion of an employee did not breach the implied term of trust and confidence. Although the employer's conduct — the demotion — was likely to damage trust and confidence, the employer had reasonable and proper cause for demoting the employee as it believed he was guilty of dishonesty. (This case shouldn't be used as an advert for unilateral demotion — it's rarely going to be fair.)

In another case, *Amnesty International v Ahmed [2009] IRLR 884*, the employer's conduct was found to be discriminatory when it refused to employ someone of northern Sudanese origin to a job researching the civil war in Sudan. However, the EAT said that the employer had reasonable and proper cause for their actions, based on risks to security and the employer's reputation. There was therefore no breach of the implied term of trust and confidence, even though there had been unlawful discrimination. This too is an unusual case. Unlawful discrimination by an employer will usually breach the implied term of trust and confidence. However, both these cases show how the employment tribunal will analyse an employer's arguments about having good reason (reasonable and proper cause) for their conduct.

What sort of things can breach the implied duty of trust and confidence?

Some of the things that can cause an employer to breach trust and confidence involve day-to-day workplace issues that go wrong. And remember that all-important 'last straw' principle that we looked at in Part 1. Even if some of the acts set out below don't breach trust and confidence by themselves, they could contribute to a series of actions which together amount to a serious breach of the implied term. What sort of things are we talking about?

Disciplinary and grievance processes

Failure to provide an impartial grievance appeal process could be, or contribute to, a breach of trust and confidence. In *Blackburn v Aldi [2013] IRLR 846*, the employee's grievance appeal was heard by the same manager who dismissed the original grievance. The EAT said this failure could be, or contribute to, a breach of trust and confidence. The right to an impartial appeal in a grievance process is an important part of the Acas code. In this case, it was also part of the employer's own procedures. The EAT couldn't see why an employer the size of Aldi would struggle to find an independent manager to hear the appeal. Very small employers might have problems finding two different managers for both grievance hearing and appeal, but this will be rare and unlikely in a large employer like Aldi.

The EAT in *Aldi* said that failing to stick to a grievance procedure might be, or contribute to, a breach of trust and confidence. That doesn't mean that every single minor breach of a grievance policy will have this effect. Some minor breaches of policy, such as failing to stick rigidly to a short timetable, are unlikely to contribute to a breach in most cases. Bigger failings, such as a complete failure to respond to a grievance, might get an employer into hot water.

Disciplinary processes should be conducted fairly and reasonably too. Issuing a severe warning in front of colleagues might breach trust and confidence. Giving first and final written warnings for lateness on consecutive days might cause problems too. Being too harsh, too soon, can come back to bite. Employers must also guard against bringing proceedings against an employee in relation to one issue, but then consider other unrelated issues as part of the process. Stick to the issue for which the employee is being disciplined.

Suspension can cause problems too if it is a knee jerk reaction in every disciplinary case. Suspension should be used only if there is 'reasonable and proper cause' for it. Other methods of preserving evidence or assisting investigation should be considered first, such as transferring the employee, and ensuring that any period of suspension is as short as possible. That analysis will add weight to any 'reasonable and proper cause' argument as and when you do suspend an employee. Employers should always ask themselves: 'Why are we doing this?'

Negative comments about an employee

Will an employer's negative comments about an employee breach trust and confidence? It depends what the comments are and where they are made. If comments are made at board level, between directors, this is the company's 'thinking aloud' process and unlikely to be a breach. There will be 'reasonable and proper cause' for negative discussions about employees between directors, or between managers and HR Professionals. An employee would have to show that there was no 'reasonable or proper cause' for the comments, which will be tricky unless the comments go way beyond what is 'reasonable and proper' in their particular situation.

Comments made by an employer in the press might be different. There are two kinds of public comment: things that are said about an employee that are untrue, and truths which are personal and confidential. Both these kinds of publication can potentially breach trust and confidence if the employee can show there was no reasonable or proper cause for comments being published. In *RDF Media v Clements [2008] IRLR 207*, the employee was a public figure in the media industry. He was being poached from one company by another in a potentially high-profile departure. The employer made various negative comments to the press, including the comment 'if you take the money you do the bloody job, it's just so dishonourable'. The High Court said a press release might be appropriate when a high-profile employee resigns. However, in this case the employer's comments were an attack on the employee's character. Whether they were true or not, the comments went beyond what was 'reasonable and proper' in that situation and were either calculated to seriously damage trust and confidence or likely to do so.

A breach of trust and confidence can be particularly problematic where they invalidate post-termination restrictions and put the business at risk. Open and frank board discussions are fine. However, employers should always guard against slanging matches against employees, especially comments that might be discriminatory or look bad if reiterated in court. Press releases should be carefully managed. There may be circumstances where an employer needs to correct misstatements in the press, but that should not go beyond what is necessary.

Overstepping the managerial mark

An employer's actions in giving instructions to employees is restricted by the duty of trust and confidence, even though employees should obey reasonable instructions. In _United Bank v Akhtar [1989] IRLR 507_, the employer used a contractual mobility clause to require an employee to move from Leeds to Birmingham on short notice. The failure to give reasonable notice breached trust and confidence in that case. In another case, _UB v Elsworthy (EAT/254/91)_, a failure to agree to put a married couple on the same shift pattern, when there was little effort needed to do so, breached trust and confidence. It meant the couple were rarely at home together and there was no reasonable or proper cause for the employer's refusal to change things around.

Employers must ensure that their decisions are fair and reasonable. Sometimes, sticking rigidly to a contract can cause problems for employers, as it did in these two cases. It's not always enough to say, 'but the contract says we can do it'.

Bonuses and pay rises

Although employers aren't usually obliged to give pay increases or bonuses, the implied duty of trust and confidence means they must treat employees fairly. If you give some employees a bonus but not others, you need to justify that decision. If the difference in treatment is unreasonable, it could breach trust and confidence. This was the situation in the *Transco* case where one employee wasn't offered the new and more favourable contract that his colleagues were offered.

The test is a little bit different in relation to discretionary bonuses. An employer doesn't have to pay what a 'reasonable employer' would have paid, but its decisions must be rational rather than arbitrary. The bonus scheme rules will be relevant here, as will the bonuses awarded to other employees at the same level. The test isn't about whether the employee's performance has been good, bad or indifferent — it's whether the employer's decision not to pay was irrational.

For example, it's probably not irrational to refuse to pay a discretionary bonus to your chief economist whose inaccurate forecasts contributed to serious financial losses. If your bonus scheme rules say bonuses are paid to attract, motivate and retain staff, it normally won't be irrational to refuse to pay a bonus to an employee who is leaving.

Employers should have clear rules about bonus schemes and pay rises. Discretion should be exercised carefully, and schemes should be transparent and fair. If a manager can't easily articulate why an employee should or shouldn't get a bonus or pay rise, it's worth probing.

Other things that can breach trust and confidence:

- Bullying and abuse by managers in the performance of their duties will breach trust and confidence. If the bullying or abuse comes from colleagues, management failure to address the situation can breach the implied term too;

- Setting unachievable targets and workloads;

- Discrimination and harassment can breach trust and confidence, such as managers making unwanted sexual advances or a failure to make reasonable adjustments for someone's disability. Remember that the tests for discrimination and breach of the implied term are separate, so although discrimination will often breach trust and confidence, there may be rare cases where it doesn't, such as the Amnesty case we looked at earlier;

- Failing to pay equal pay to an employee;

- Conducting a consultation process (redundancy, TUPE, for example) in an aggressive or underhand way, such as providing false information or acting in bad faith by deliberately concealing information;

- Underhand behaviour leading up to a change in an employee's terms and conditions, although remember we said that giving notice itself is unlikely to breach trust and confidence;

- Giving a misleading or inaccurate reference, although since most references are given after employment ends, it wouldn't normally lead to a constructive dismissal claim.

What if the employee breaches trust and confidence?

The duty of trust and confidence is a mutual one, so it applies to employees in the same way as employers. It is rarely used by employers though. Most choose to follow their own disciplinary processes in the event of a contractual breach or bad behaviour by an employee.

An employee's breach of trust and confidence can be a useful tool for employers in constructive dismissal claims. Where the employee has already breached the implied term of trust and confidence themselves, this might impact on their constructive dismissal claim. This happened in the *RDF Media v Clements* case we discussed earlier. Although the employer's unreasonable press comments breached trust and confidence, the employee had already breached the duty by his own behaviour in disclosing confidential information to his new employer. As a result, the High Court said he couldn't claim constructive dismissal. This meant that his restrictive covenants and notice period were enforceable by the employer.

This might not always be the case though. In other High Court cases (*Tullett Prebon v BGC Brokers [2011] IRLR 420* and *Brandeaux Advisors v Chadwick [2011] IRLR 224*) the judges took a different approach. They said that if an employee breaches the employment contract, but the employer doesn't terminate the contract in response, then employment continues as normal. That means that an employee can choose to resign in response to a subsequent fundamental breach by the employer. The EAT looked at these and other cases in *Atkinson v Community Gateway Association [2014] IRLR 834*. The EAT agreed that the contract of employment continues as normal unless one party accept the other's breach (by resigning or dismissing the other). However, the

EAT noted that if the employee was originally at fault, but then brought a successful constructive dismissal case, the tribunal would consider reducing compensation. If the employer could establish that the employee would have been fairly dismissed had they known about a repudiatory breach at the time, compensation could be reduced by up to 100 per cent.

Can an employer repair a repudiatory breach?

In short, no. Once an employer has fundamentally breached an employee's contract, there is no going back. The employee's actions alone will decide what happens next. Either they waive the breach and affirm the contract or choose to consider that the employment relationship has finished. What the employer does now is irrelevant.

The exception to this is in cases of anticipatory breach, where the breach hasn't yet happened. An employer can correct an anticipatory breach at any point before the employee accepts it. Let's say an employer tells an employee that he will have to move offices and take a demotion in a month's time. Realising their grave error, the employer calls the employee in the next day and says none of those things will happen after all. The anticipatory breach has been cured. The breach itself will never happen. Provided the employee didn't do anything to accept the anticipatory breach — such as resigning — before it was withdrawn, then the employer is in the clear.

Although there is a potential Get Out of Jail Free card for anticipatory breaches, it's better to avoid them occurring in the first place. As always in employment law, prevention is better than cure.

5. What else can amount to a repudiatory breach?

We've already looked at some practical examples of repudiatory breaches in relation to trust and confidence. What else can create a really serious breach that an employee can act on? It's helpful to know what sort of things have been found by the courts to be a repudiatory breach. This can help employers to avoid similar events happening in their own workplaces.

- Reducing an employee's pay unilaterally will usually be a repudiatory breach of their employment contract. It shows that the employer doesn't intend to be bound by the contractual terms about the employee's pay. It is also likely to breach the implied term of trust and confidence between employer and employee.

- Unilaterally changing an employee's duties from the duties contained in their employment contract and job description (or other terms that have arisen in practice but aren't in writing). Flexibility clauses might give the employer some wriggle room but will never provide free rein to request any duties whatsoever of the employee.

- Discrimination will usually be a repudiatory breach of contract, often based on a breach of trust and confidence. The courts have found that a discriminatory refusal to allow a woman to return to work part time was a repudiatory breach of contract. So too was less favourable treatment of a disabled employee and failure to make reasonable adjustments by reducing her sick pay. Both employees were entitled to resign and claim constructive dismissal.

- Failing to allow an employee the opportunity to complain about workplace issues via a grievance procedure. Badly handled grievances won't always create a repudiatory breach of contract — it will depend on the facts — but does create risk.

- Handling disciplinary matters badly, including communicating unreasonable allegations and knee jerk suspension. In *Gogay v Hertfordshire*

County Council [2000] IRLR 703, the employer suspended a care worker for sexual abuse of a child in her care. These allegations were based on ambiguous remarks made by a child with learning difficulties. The allegations were unfounded. The suspension had been a knee jerk reaction and was unjustified, and it breached trust and confidence. The employer in this case should have made further inquiries about the allegations and their merit before suspending the employee.

- Demoting an employee. As well as a breach of trust and confidence, demotion is likely to be a breach of the express term in the employee's contract about the job that they are employed to do.

- Unbearable work environments can constitute a breach trust and confidence, even in industries where high pressure is expected and management is known to be aggressive. In *Horkulak v Cantor Fitzgerald International [2003] IRLR 756*, the employee was a senior managing director. He reported to the company president and CEO. He was paid £250,000 per year plus a bonus. He resigned and claimed constructive dismissal due to the CEO's bullying and abusive behaviour.

The employer agreed that the CEO had a forceful management style and used bad language. However, they said it was a high-pressure workplace where pay was high and bad language commonplace. They said the employee left because he couldn't handle the pressure of the job rather than because of the CEO's behaviour. The High Court said that the CEO's behaviour breached trust and confidence. Frequent use of bad language didn't remove or reduce its impact or power to offend. There is no different standard of conduct for an employer that pays well.

Part 3

Responding to the breach

In the earlier sections of this book, we looked in detail at repudiatory breaches of contract. It is the repudiatory breach which entitles the employee to resign without notice and claim they were dismissed. But the breach itself doesn't create the constructive dismissal. There is only a dismissal if the employee resigns in response to the breach.

When faced with a repudiatory breach, the employee has two choices:

- 'Accept' the breach and treat the contract as finished by resigning; or

- 'Affirm' the contract by waiving (ignoring) the breach and continuing in employment.

6. 'Accepting' the breach

In order to bring a constructive dismissal claim, the employee must 'accept' the breach, and act on it by resigning. The idea that a repudiatory breach alone is not enough — and the employee must accept that breach — was made clear by the Supreme Court in the case of *Société Générale, London Branch v Geys [2013] IRLR 122.*

The Geys case

The employee was a managing director at the bank's London branch. His contract said that his employment could be terminated on three months' notice. It also said a severance payment would be made in 'no fault' terminations. The bank's handbook, which was incorporated into employee contracts, also said that the employee's employment could be terminated immediately by paying him a payment in lieu of notice (PILON).

On 29 November, the employee was told that his employment would terminate immediately. He was given a letter, asked to clear his desk and was escorted from the building. No PILON was paid to the employee at this stage. Lawyer letters between the parties ensued, primarily discussing the value of the 'no fault' termination payment which was due. On 18 December, the sum of £32,000 was paid into the employee's bank account with no explanation about what it was or how it was calculated. The employee became aware of the payment later in December.

It was better for the employee if his dismissal date fell in January rather than December due to bonus and benefit calculations. In early January, the employee's lawyers wrote to the bank affirming his employment contract. A couple of days later the bank wrote to the employee saying he had been given notice on 29 November and his PILON was paid on 18 December. In dispute over the value of his termination payment, and with the termination date being an important factor, the employee brought claims of wrongful dismissal and breach of contract. The difference in potential calculations ran into several million Euro.

What the courts said

The High Court said the employee's employment terminated on 6 January when he received the bank's letter. This was the first time the employer had told him that they were exercising the terms of the handbook about immediate termination. The employer appealed, saying their repudiatory breach (dismissing the employee without paying a PILON) on 29 November automatically ended the employment contract and the employee could not choose whether to accept that breach.

The Supreme Court agreed with the High Court. The employee's employment ended on 6 January. His actions after the employer's repudiatory breach clearly affirmed the contract. Until the employer had validly exercised its contractual right to terminate in lieu of notice — by paying the PILON and writing to the employee to explain their actions — his employment continued, until early January. As a result, he was entitled to the higher termination payment.

It's hard to feel too much sympathy with an employee who is arguing about how many millions they are owed, but there are important legal principles here. The first, and obvious, one is to follow your own contractual procedures. Had the employer in this case properly exercised its contractual right to immediate termination at the outset (by telling the employee the contractual basis for termination and paying him a PILON), the termination date would have been November when he was walked off the premises. The lower payment would have applied.

More relevant to constructive dismissal though, the Supreme Court confirmed that it is the employee's action (in accepting the breach and resigning) which creates the dismissal rather than the breach itself. The ball is firmly in the employee's court.

What must the employee tell the employer?

The employee doesn't have to tell the employer directly what they are doing in relation to a serious breach. In *Mr Auto Clutch Centres v Blakemore (UKEAT/0509/13)*, the Employment Appeal Tribunal said that bringing a claim for constructive unfair dismissal was 'accepting' the employer's breach and acting on it. The employee didn't need to tell his employer in advance. Sometimes, the first an employer will know about a constructive dismissal claim will be the arrival of the ET1.

Employee's action must be 'unequivocal'

If the employee wants to accept the breach (and act on it by resigning) then they need to be unequivocal about it. 'Unequivocal' just means 'clear'. If the employee's actions aren't clear, they may unintentionally be found to have waived the breach and affirmed the employment contract.

It can be tricky to establish what that clarity looks like in practice. If an employee resigns, it's pretty clear that they mean business. But what about actions short of resignation? In *Atlantic Air v Hoff (UKEAT/0602/07)*, the employee was abused by the company's owner at a meeting on 5 March, a repudiatory breach of contract. There were three possible dates when the employee accepted the employer's breach:

- At the meeting itself when he told his employer 'I am not taking this shit';

- 8 March, when he piloted a flight for another company; and

- 14 March, when his solicitor wrote to the employer accepting the breach of contract and giving his resignation.

It was an important point in this case because the employee's claim form would only be in time if the last date were applicable. The EAT said the employee had not unequivocally accepted the employer's breach until 14 March. Though his words of 5 March seemed clear, they were said in the heat of the moment. It would not have been reasonable to assume these words were his formal resignation. Nor was doing a day's work for a third party accepting the breach. The employee could have done that and still complied with his principal contract with the employer. Neither of these events were clear enough to be unequivocal acceptance of a breach.

The EAT said things might have been different if the employee had signed an exclusive employment contract with a third party on 8 March. That would be different and indicate unequivocal acceptance of the original employer's breach by agreeing to work exclusively for someone else.

7. Waiving the breach and 'affirming' the contract

If there is a serious breach of contract by the employer, the employee can waive (or ignore) the breach. In waiving a breach, an employee will 'affirm' the contract, showing they intend to continue in employment regardless.

Even if an employee has no intention of ignoring a breach, they may accidentally affirm their contract of employment if they wait too long before acting. This is because affirming a contract can be express or implied. An employee theoretically might say to their employer: 'I know you've seriously breached my contract, but I need the money so I'm carrying on in employment regardless.' This would be an express waiver of a repudiatory breach. More often, though, affirmation of a contract (by waiving a breach) will be implied by what the employee does, rather than anything they expressly say.

What does affirmation look like?

The employee must do one of two things:

- Act in a way which shows that they consider the employment contract to be continuing; or

- Call on the employer to act in accordance with the employment contract which will also show that they consider the employment contract to remain in place.

What do these things look like in real life? Let's say an employee shows up for work the day after a repudiatory breach. Going to work means that the employee is behaving in a way which demonstrates the employment contract continues. Will that mean the employee has affirmed the contract and waived the breach simply by turning up for work? And what if the employee is paid in the days or weeks following a breach. Will accepting their salary and continuing to work affirm the contract too? In both these cases there is some delay, which necessarily involves the employment contract continuing in the meantime. Will that kind of delay affirm the employment contract and scupper a constructive dismissal claim?

Depending on the facts, the courts will usually be flexible about some delay. It is important for the employee to make their objections clear even if they delay before taking further action. In *Marriott v Oxford and District Cooperative Society [1970] 1 QB 186*, the employee was a foreman. The business was in financial difficulty and the employee was asked to take a demotion with reduced pay. The employee objected, and a higher level of reduced pay was offered. The employee still objected to the demotion. In the meantime, he applied for another job and he left his original employment within a few weeks. He claimed a redundancy payment, saying that his termination was not consensual. The Court of Appeal said that the employer had unilaterally terminated the employee's contract. Under the prevailing redundancy laws, the employee was entitled to a redundancy payment. The employee had clearly objected to the demotion (a serious breach of contract) and he was not considered to have waived the breach just by continuing in employment and taking his pay for a few weeks. That is the case even if the employee's main aim is to secure another job before jumping ship.

What sort of delay will be too long?

Although some delay won't necessarily affirm an employment contract, an employee cannot hang around forever. Sadly, there are no hard and fast rules here. The main thing to appreciate is that any delay itself isn't the issue. It's whether that delay indicates any express or implied affirmation. Too much delay and a tribunal might consider that is evidence of affirmation depending on the other facts of the case.

It isn't easy for an employer to look at a set of facts and assess what level of delay will be fatal to a constructive dismissal claim. Even Court of Appeal judges in the same case have taken different views on the same set of facts. In *Buckland v Bournemouth University [2010] IRLR 445*, the majority of judges said that employment tribunals could be 'reasonably robust' when looking at how an employee behaves. They said an employee who doesn't make their position clear at the outset can't carry on for long without losing the option of resigning, especially where an employer has taken steps to make things better. However, another judge in the same case noted that employees are often in an unenviable position, having to weigh up the need to pay the bills with the risk that any delay might indicate affirmation. This judge said that, in an ideal world, an employee might want to stay on 'for a bit' while they considered their position. He accepted that this was unlikely in practice and so waiver will always depend on the facts in each case.

There have been harsh cases. In *Fereday v South Staffordshire NHS Trust (UKEAT/0513/10/ZT)*, an employee delayed his resignation for six weeks while he was off sick. During that period, he accepted sick pay, asked for it to be extended, and raised queries about a change in job title. The EAT said he had affirmed his contract. Other cases appear more measured. In *Chindove v Morrisons (UKEAT/0201/13/BA)*, the EAT said that it was an employee's conduct that was relevant rather than timing. They said delay might be easier to understand (and less likely to indicate affirmation) if the employee is on sick leave rather than at work. There may also be other reasons why an employee delays raising objections, for example if they are waiting for more information from their employer before raising a grievance.

Working under protest

Sometimes, an employee might try to buy themselves time by continuing to work after a breach whilst saying expressly that they are working under protest. In theory, provided they have made it clear that they are not waiving the breach, or are continuing in work to allow the employer to put things right, then some delay may not be fatal. But even in this situation, there will come a time where the employee must either take action or accept the risk that their behaviour indicates waiver of the breach after all.

In the classic case of _Hogg v Dover College [1990] ICR 39_, the employee was unilaterally demoted resulting in a 50% pay decrease. He agreed to work to the new terms but reserved his right to bring an unfair dismissal claim. The EAT said the demotion was either a dismissal and re-engagement or a fundamental breach of contract which the employee had accepted giving rise to a constructive dismissal claim. The employee hadn't affirmed the contract by agreeing to work to new terms because there was nothing of the old contract left to affirm. He was employed on completely new terms but could bring a claim for constructive or other unfair dismissal even though he continued in employment.

Cases where delay was not an issue

Munchkins Restaurant v Karmazyn [2010] EWCA Civ 1163: The employees said they had put up with intolerable sexual harassment for years. They were vulnerable migrant workers who were under great financial pressure to continue working. They coped with the situation until their assistant manager left, after which they all resigned within three months. The EAT said that the women's delay was reasonable. Their situation was like a victim of domestic violence: 'putting up with it does not make it welcome'.

Post Office v Roberts [1980] IRLR 347: An employee delayed resigning for six weeks while her trade union representative investigated the issue.

Bashir v Brillo [1979] IRLR 295: A delay of 10 weeks wasn't fatal when the employee was off sick.

El-Hoshi v Pizza Express (UKEAT/0857/03):
An assistant manager was ordered to work in the
kitchens which he found humiliating. He went
off sick and received two months' sick pay before
resigning. The delay wasn't fatal. The employee
had never worked in the new role, so delay was a
neutral factor. He had continued to complain to
the employer while he was off sick about the lack of
action against his manager.

Abbey National v Robinson (UKEAT/743/99):
This case is a reminder about how last straws
can come into play and revive an employee's
right to rely on earlier, waived, breaches. This
case involved sexual harassment by a manager.
The employee's complaints were upheld but she
was told her manager would not be transferred
and she would be moved instead (arguably a
repudiatory breach). The employer toyed for a
year with how to bring the employee back to
work, eventually offering her a job which was
then revoked without explanation. Revoking the
job offer was the last straw and the delay of a year
was not too long to bring a claim.

Cases where delay was too long

WE Cox Toner v Crook [1981] IRLR 443: A
director delayed seven months before resigning
after allegations by colleagues, even though he

had protested about the situation for much of that period.

Quigley v University of St Andrews (UKEATS/0025/05): The employee delayed for two months before resigning so he could take legal advice from a solicitor. The employee claimed he couldn't have affirmed the contract without knowing his legal rights. The EAT disagreed and said the delay meant he had affirmed the contract.

Colomar Mari v Reuters (UKEAT/0539/13/MC): In this case, 18 months' delay was too long. The employee had accepted 39 weeks of sick pay and said she was too ill to take action. Although this argument was rejected, the EAT said that there may be cases where an employee doesn't take action because they are too sick and accepting sick pay might not always contribute to any arguments about affirmation of contract.

Does the employer's behaviour have to be the only reason for resignation?

Provided the employer's breach played a part in the decision to leave, that is enough for a constructive dismissal claim. In *Logan v Celyn House (UKEAT/0069/12/JOJ)*, an employee resigned on two bases: bullying, which was later found to be imagined, and a failure to pay contractual sick pay which she had raised as a grievance. The employment tribunal decided the main reason she resigned was the bullying. Even though the failure to pay sick pay was a fundamental breach of contract, her constructive dismissal claim failed because it wasn't her main reason for resigning. The EAT disagreed. Once a fundamental breach has been identified, that breach just needs to be one of the reasons for resigning. It doesn't have to be the main or the only reason.

Sometimes, an employee's challenging private life might appear to be the reason for resignation rather than any breach. In *Wright v North Ayrshire Council [2014] IRLR 4*, the employer had seriously breached the employee's contract by failing to respond properly to grievances. The employee was a carer for her sick mother, who died at around the same time her partner suffered a stroke. The employment tribunal said 'the effective cause' of her resignation was her inability to juggle her job and personal circumstances. The EAT disagreed. They said the relevant issue wasn't the 'effective cause' of her resignation, but whether the breach had played a part in it. The case was sent back to the tribunal to look at this issue again.

Does the employee have to say why they are leaving?

In short, no. The key to a constructive dismissal claim is resigning in response to the employer's repudiatory breach, rather than what they have said about that resignation. In *Weathersfield v Sargent [1999] IRLR 94*, the employee was white and got a receptionist's job at a car rental firm. She was told that the company had a policy of telling potential customers who were from ethnic minorities that there were no hire cars available. This upset the employee and made her position untenable. She rang the employer to say she was leaving but didn't tell them the reason. The Court of Appeal overruled previous EAT case law and said this did not defeat her constructive dismissal claim. The employee had been put in an embarrassing and impossible position. It was understandable that she didn't want to have that discussion with her employer. The Court noted that the employee's resignation, including reasons given, will form just one element of the evidence the tribunal considers when deciding whether the breach was a factor in the resignation. Sometimes, a failure to pass comment might be relevant to whether the resignation was a response to any breach, but it wasn't here.

Sometimes, an employee might be nervous about a bad reference and give a misleadingly positive resignation letter. Even that doesn't necessarily defeat a constructive dismissal claim. In *Nicholson v Hazel House Nursing Home (UKEAT/0241/15/LA)*, the employee's shifts were changed after she announced her pregnancy. The reduction in hours meant that she only qualified for statutory maternity allowance instead of statutory maternity pay. She resigned after her grievance was dismissed. Her resignation letter didn't mention the grievance and gave other reasons for resigning, including a desire to spend time with her baby. She did this because she didn't want to get a negative reference. She then brought a constructive dismissal claim. The employment tribunal said she had not been constructively dismissed but the EAT overturned that decision. The EAT said there was no requirement to raise the failed grievance in the resignation letter and it was an error of law for the tribunal to say this was determinative.

Resigning with notice

In Part 1 we touched on the fact that employees must be entitled to resign without notice, even if they go on to give notice before leaving. Giving notice will not necessarily be fatal to a constructive dismissal claim. Section 95(1)(c) the *Employment Rights Act 1996* specifically refers to constructive dismissals 'with or without notice'.

In the rare case where an employee gives longer notice than necessary, that might be evidence that the employee has waived the breach. Going above and beyond the contract can only be consistent with affirming it. There will always be exceptions to any rule, such as the lecturer who deliberately gave long notice to preserve his students' academic best interests in *Buckland v Bournemouth University [2010] IRLR 445.*

In most cases, an employee's decision to give notice will just be one part of a bigger picture. It is the employment tribunal's job to consider that fact along with the rest of the evidence. Giving notice will not necessarily be fatal.

Part 4
Beyond the breach

So far in this book, the dismissals we have talked about involve the employer's behaviour towards an employee — a fundamental breach of contract that entitles the employee to resign and claim constructive dismissal. But constructive dismissals can be based on other things too: the behaviour of a colleague, for example, or the actions of a third party.

8. Actions of others

Behaviour of colleagues or managers

In an employment context, an employer can be held responsible for the acts or omissions of its employees which take place during employment. This can include things like bullying and harassment, violent assaults or discriminatory acts. It can also cover cases where employees misuse their position. Section 109(1) of the *Equality Act 2010* makes employers responsible for the discriminatory acts of their employees. The employer can only escape liability if it can show that it has taken all reasonable steps to prevent that discrimination taking place.

The test is whether the employer is vicariously liable for the actions of the manager or colleague. A constructive dismissal can be based on the actions of a manager, even if that person wouldn't usually have the authority to dismiss the employee. In *Hilton International Hotels v Protopapa [1990] IRLR 316*, the employee was severely reprimanded by her supervisor in front of other employees. The employment tribunal said she had been constructively dismissed. The reprimand had been unjustified, officious and insensitive. The employee felt so humiliated and degraded that it breached the implied term of trust and confidence. The employer appealed, saying that the supervisor didn't have the authority to dismiss which meant the employee couldn't have been constructively dismissed.

The Employment Appeal Tribunal said the employer was responsible for the acts of their employees if the employee was doing their job and, in doing so, did something which constituted a fundamental breach of an employee's contract. The supervisor had been acting within the general scope of her job when reprimanding the employee, so the employer was liable. The employee had been constructively dismissed.

Behaviour towards someone else

Usually, an employee complains about behaviour directed at themselves. Constructive dismissal claims can also be based on behaviour an employer directs at others. Remember the test that we talked about in Part 2 — trust and confidence can be broken by '*conduct that is likely to destroy trust and confidence between employer and employee*'. It doesn't have to be action directed specifically at an individual employee. Sometimes an employer's actions towards someone else will be relevant.

An employee can bring a claim against an employer in relation to their mistreatment of other employees. In *Hunter v Timber Components (UKEATS/0025/09)*, the employee resigned because the owner's son was bullying and harassing other employees. The employee brought a claim for constructive dismissal. He lost his case on the facts, but the EAT confirmed that an employer's conduct towards one employee might breach the implied term of trust and confidence with another. That could be behaviour towards a fellow employee or even behaviour towards a third party. Sometimes throwing a stone creates bigger ripples than you might expect.

Behaviour by third parties

Employers can be responsible for third-party behaviour in some situations. There isn't a definitive test for this, but the factors set out below will be relevant:

- Was the third party paid by the employer to provide a service or do a job?

- Did the activity done by the third party benefit the employer?

- Was the third party's action 'reasonably incidental' (closely connected) to the duties they were carrying out for the employer?

- Could the employer control what was done by the third party and how it was done?

- Could the employer choose who did the third-party activity?

- Could the employer suspend or stop the activity the third party was doing?

- Was the wrongdoing authorised by the employer, either expressly or impliedly?

- Was the wrongdoing an authorised way of doing an authorised task or job?

- Was the wrongdoing something that the third party wasn't required to do, or had been forbidden to do?

The questions show that the issue here is how much control the employer has over the third party and their behaviour. In *De Clare Johnson v MYA Consulting (UKEAT/0306/07)*, the employer was held responsible for the actions of the managing director's husband. The employee worked as a housekeeper for the catering and hotelkeeping consultancy service run from the managing director's home. Her husband, who didn't work for the business, behaved badly towards the employee. He shouted and screamed at her about tasks or perceived infractions, including cleaning. The employment tribunal found that the husband's action had breached trust and confidence. The employer appealed, saying it wasn't responsible for the actions of the managing director's husband.

The EAT said the employer was responsible. The events took place at work in relation to tasks the employee was employed to do and for which she was paid. The cleaning tasks in question benefitted the company. The company could control what cleaning was to be done, how and by whom, and was able to select who should do it. The Employment Appeal Tribunal found that the husband had implied authority to give the employee instructions.

The EAT also said that an employer has a duty to provide a suitable working environment. The employee's workplace should have been free from shouting or bad behaviour by someone in the same building who was closely connected to the managing director. There was an implied duty on the employer to protect the employee from being badly treated by the husband who lived in the employee's workplace.

This was a very specific case where the wrongdoer lived in the employee's workplace. However, the principle can be extended to other situations where third parties are closely connected to the workplace and where bad or bullying behaviour is ignored or condoned. Employers should address any bad behaviour from third parties who come into the workplace.

Grievances

The Acas code of practice does not stipulate that that an employer must follow a grievance process for a former employee and there isn't any case law on this issue yet. Does this mean employers can just ignore a grievance lodged by an aggrieved ex-employee that alludes to a constructive dismissal? Best practice is to deal with any grievance that is lodged. It allows an employer to potentially resolve the issue or right any wrongdoing before matters end up in an employment tribunal. It won't make a good impression on an employment judge if an employer refuses to deal with a grievance simply because there is no legal requirement to do so. Most employees will be advised to raise a grievance before lodging proceedings, to cover their backs. Employers should deal with such grievances meticulously.

9. Compensation — how much is a constructive dismissal worth?

There are two main claims to consider in relation to constructive dismissals: compensation for breach of contract and compensation for unfair dismissal.

Breach of contract

Remember that a constructive dismissal claim is based on a breach of contract — the fundamental breach of contract that entitles the employee to resign and say they were dismissed. Any employee, regardless of how long they have been employed, can bring a breach of contract claim in response to that breach. An employee can choose to bring this claim in the employment tribunal — which caps compensation at £25,000 — or in the civil courts, where compensation is uncapped.

Most employees who bring constructive dismissal claims resign without notice. Compensation for that breach — the lack of notice — will reflect what they would have received had they worked, or been paid in lieu of, their notice. This will be a net figure for their contractual notice period.

The law says that employees in this situation must 'mitigate their loss', which means they must take reasonable steps to get a new job if one is available. Any money they earn in their notice period will be offset against what the employer should pay in damages. If someone's contractual notice period is three months, and they get a job after one month, then any money which they have earned in the new job should be deducted from the amount claimed for their notice period. Remember that a new job might not pay the same as the original job, so the dismissing employer would be expected to make up the shortfall for any notice period.

Unfair dismissal

If an employee has two years' continuous service, then they can also bring an unfair dismissal claim. The same basic rules about compensation for unfair dismissal apply to constructive unfair dismissals. An employee may claim:

- An order for reinstatement or reengagement

- A basic award

- A compensatory award.

Reinstatement and reengagement

Reinstatement orders require the employer to treat the employee as if they had never been dismissed, reinstating them to their previous job on the same terms and conditions with no loss of pay in the interim period. Reengagement orders require an employer to reemploy the employee to a comparable job or one which is otherwise suitable, on terms which are as favourable if that's reasonably practicable.

These orders are rare in the best of circumstances, being made in less than 1 per cent of cases. In each case an employment tribunal will have to consider two things: whether the employee wants to be taken back on and whether it's practicable for the employer to comply with the order. These orders are even less likely in constructive dismissal cases where relationships have broken down and the employment contract has been breached. An employee is unlikely to request this kind of order. If they did, an employment tribunal is unlikely to think it is practicable to put an employee back to work in a business that has fundamentally breached their contract. Instead they would award compensation, a basic award and a compensatory award.

Basic award

This is an award based on age, length of service and gross weekly pay (capped at £538 from April 2020). It is calculated in the same way as statutory redundancy pay and is designed to compensate the employee for the loss of job security.

Compensatory award

The employee can recover any losses which flow from the dismissal subject to a statutory cap which is currently £88,519. An employment tribunal will have to decide what compensation is 'just and equitable' in relation to the particular case. Case law has found that 'loss' is limited to financial losses which result from the dismissal. This might include loss of earnings if the employee has spent a period of time unemployed or if they have secured new employment on lower pay. It might also include loss of pension and other benefits, bonus and commission, and even any expenses the employee has incurred in looking for new work.

Getting around the compensation cap

The statutory cap on unfair dismissal compensation is precisely why a crafty employee might prefer to bring a claim relating to their dismissal as a breach of contract claim in the civil courts rather than an unfair dismissal in the employment tribunal. And it makes sense in constructive dismissal cases — if a fundamental breach of contract (the constructive dismissal) causes loss, it can technically form the basis of a breach of contract claim. And remember that damages for breach of contract claims in the civil courts are uncapped.

Case law has now established that employees cannot get around the statutory cap by bringing a breach of contract claim instead of a claim for constructive unfair dismissal. The basic premise is that the government has created a specific process for unfair dismissal — with a capped remedy — and employees will not be allowed to circumvent it. Case law has confirmed that any kind of breach which is linked to dismissal — breach of the implied term of trust and confidence which ends in a constructive dismissal claim, or breach of a contractual disciplinary policy in a 'normal' dismissal — has to be dealt with under the unfair dismissal laws rather than breach of contract.

What cannot be claimed in the compensatory award?

An employee cannot claim compensation for hurt feelings associated with the dismissal or how it happened. In a case called *Dunnachie v Kingston Upon Hull City Council [2004] IRLR 727*, the House of Lords confirmed that employees cannot claim injury to feelings as part of an unfair dismissal claim. Compensation is based on financial losses only. In that case, the employee was bullied by his manager and went off with stress before being dismissed and bringing a claim for unfair dismissal. He claimed compensation for damage to family life and loss of professional status as well as financial losses. He was awarded injury to feelings by the employment tribunal, but the House of Lords overturned the decision, saying the employee could only claim financial losses.

Except in very exceptional circumstances, employees cannot claim 'stigma damages' - compensation for the unemployability an employee might suffer as a result of being associated with a certain employer. In the latter situation though, an employment tribunal might award compensation for a longer period if an employee can show they are unable to secure work.

Stigma damages — the exception to the rule

There is a very narrow exception to the rule on 'stigma damages' which can be claimed as a separate claim for breach of contract. *Malik v Bank of Credit and Commerce International [1997] IRLR 462* involved the fallout from the demise of the BCCI bank which had conducted business in a corrupt manner. Employees brought breach of contract claims in the High Court. They said that their association with the bank meant they were unable to get jobs in the financial sector because their honesty and integrity was tainted by their employment with the bank.

The House of Lords found that the bank had conducted itself in a way which was likely to seriously damage or destroy trust and confidence, which caused the employee loss of reputation and employability. The employees won their claims by showing that they were unable to secure alternative work as a result of the stigma attached to working for the demised bank.

These cases will be extremely rare but dishonest and corrupt employers might find that employees are able to get around the compensation cap on unfair dismissal.

What about other sorts of breach of contract claim?

An employee can still bring a claim for breach of contract if a breach which occurs before dismissal causes loss. The important question is whether the loss in question flows from the dismissal (or constructive dismissal) itself or another breach of contract which came before it. The former will be swept up in any unfair dismissal claim; the latter can be brought as a separate breach of contract claim.

In *Eastwood and Williams v Magnox Electric plc [2004] IRLR 733*, the employee's manager didn't like him and bore a grudge against him. The manager started disciplinary proceedings and encouraged other employees to provide false statements in support of those allegations. One employee was threatened with disciplinary action themselves if they didn't provide a false statement. Both employees were eventually dismissed, and each had developed depression in the intervening period. They brought unfair dismissal claims which the employer settled (they paid money in return for the employees withdrawing their unfair dismissal claims).

Both employees then brought breach of contract and negligence claims, saying they had suffered personal injury (the depression) as a result of the conduct of the managers who ran the dismissal process. Financial losses flowed from that pre-dismissal breach of contract (the managers' conduct) when their sick pay ran out and they received no pay.

In the House of Lords, this case was joined with another separate case where an employee had already won his unfair dismissal claim. In that case, the employment tribunal had found that the employer's disciplinary process had been breached. The employee then brought a separate claim in the High Court for breach of contract and negligence. He said he had developed a psychiatric injury as a result of the employer's failure to investigate the allegations properly and conduct the disciplinary process fairly. Both cases went in front of the House of Lords together to decide whether their personal injury claims could continue separately from any unfair dismissal proceedings (which had either settled or concluded).

The House of Lords said that an employee has the right to pursue a separate claim if it has arisen before the dismissal itself. An employer's actions before dismissal won't usually result in financial loss but in some cases it might — suspension, for example, or a psychiatric injury or other illness caused by pre-dismissal treatment. In these cases, the employees had suffered loss as a result of pre-dismissal breaches which they could action separately as personal injury claims.

It's worth noting that an employee can't claim 'double recovery' if they bring more than one case. If there is an overlap between the financial losses sought in difference legal claims (loss of earnings for example) then they will not be allowed to claim those losses twice.

Does *Polkey* apply to constructive dismissals?

The principle of a 'Polkey deduction' stems from *Polkey v AE Dayton Services [1987] IRLR 503*, a case involving a dismissal which was procedurally unfair. In that case, the House of Lords confirmed the principle that unfair dismissal compensation can be reduced, potentially to zero, if an employee would have been dismissed anyway had a fair procedure been followed. The employment tribunal must decide by how much to reduce compensation based on the facts of the case. The case of *Gover v Propertycare [2006] ICR 1073* showed how this principle might apply to a constructive dismissal. The employer imposed a less favourable commission structure on employees without consultation. The employment tribunal found that the employees had been constructively dismissed. However, they limited the employees' compensation to four months' pay. It would have taken the employer four months to consult fairly on the changes, and the employees would have refused the new contracts anyway. The Court of Appeal confirmed that the tribunal's assessment of compensation, including the reduction, was lawful.

Contributory fault

It might seem odd for an employment tribunal to apportion fault to an employee who has been on the end of an employer's fundamental breach of contract. It will be rare but *Shipperley v Nucleus Information Systems (UKEAT/0340/06)* shows how an employee's conduct might be relevant to compensation in a constructive dismissal claim. The employee wasn't paid his wages, which was a repudiatory breach of contract. The employee resigned and won his claim for constructive dismissal. However, the employment tribunal found that the employee's behaviour had destabilised the company and led to the company being unable to pay his wages. They had no option but to find he had been constructively dismissed, but they were entitled to reduce compensation because of his conduct.

APPENDIX
Top Constructive Dismissal Cases

Western Excavating Ltd v Sharp [1978] ICR 221

Establishing constructive dismissal – what is the correct test?

This case is the leading authority on constructive dismissal and sets out the test that must be satisfied for a successful constructive dismissal claim.

Western Excavating had a policy that if you worked overtime you could take time off in lieu. Mr Sharp requested 3 hours off and was refused. He decided to take the leave anyway. The next day he was dismissed by the foreman. He appealed and his dismissal was overturned and replaced with a 5-day unpaid suspension.

This put Mr Sharp in real financial difficulty. He visited the welfare officer to request an advance on his holiday pay or a loan, both were refused. He resigned so that he was able to collect his accrued holiday pay immediately. He brought a claim for constructive dismissal.

The industrial tribunal held that Mr Sharp had been constructively dismissed and that the company should have "leant over backwards" to assist him. The EAT agreed.

The Court of Appeal considered whether the correct test was the breach of contract test, or the unreasonable test. The court favoured the 'contract test', with Lord Denning saying:

"If the employer is guilty of conduct which is a significant breach going to the root of the contract of employment, or which shows that the employer no longer intends to be bound by one or more of the essential terms of the contract, then the employee is entitled to treat himself as discharged from any further performance. If he does so, then he terminates the contract by reason of the employer's conduct."

The principles derived from this case set out the test for establishing constructive dismissal:

1. there has been a repudiatory breach by the employer

2. the employee has accepted the breach

3. the employee has resigned in response to the breach

4. the employee did not delay in resigning, so as to have affirmed the breach

Société Générale, London Branch v Geys [2013] IRLR 122

'Accepting' the breach

Mr Geys was a managing director at the bank's London branch. His contract provided that his employment could be terminated on three months' written notice. There was a PILON clause as well as a provision for a severance payment in 'no-fault' circumstances.

On 29 November, Mr Geys was told his employment would terminate "with immediate effect" and he was escorted from the building. No PILON was paid to the employee at this stage. Lawyer letters between the parties ensued, primarily discussing the value of the 'no fault' termination payment which was due.

On 18 December, £32,000 was paid into the Mr Geys' bank account with no explanation about what it was or how it was calculated. Mr Geys became aware of the payment later in December.

On 2 January, Mr Geys' lawyers wrote to the bank stating that he had decided to affirm the contract. On 6 January, Mr Geys received a letter stating the details of his termination and highlighting that the payment made on 18 December was his PILON.

There was a dispute over the date of termination, Mr Geys contended his employment ended on 6 January and the bank stating that notice was given on 29 November and that employment had automatically terminated on that date. It was more beneficial for Mr Geys if his dismissal date fell in January rather than November/December due to bonus and benefit calculations. He would be entitled to substantially more money if his termination date was in January. Mr Geys brought a claim for wrongful dismissal and breach of contract.

The High Court said that Mr Geys' employment terminated on 6 January when he received the bank's letter. This was the first time the bank had told him that they were exercising their right to make a payment in lieu of notice and set out the details. Under his contract he was entitled to proper written notice of termination, and he did not receive that until January.

The bank appealed, saying their repudiatory breach (dismissing the employee without paying a

PILON) on 29 November automatically ended the employment contract and the employee could not choose whether to accept that breach.

However, the Supreme Court agreed with the High Court. There are two theories about when the termination of an employment contract takes place, following a repudiatory breach. The 'automatic theory' says that the termination takes effect automatically following the repudiation. The 'elective theory' says that the termination does not take place until the other party has accepted the breach.

The issue before the Supreme Court was which theory is correct and should be followed? The court decided that the 'elective theory' was the correct one – the breach must be accepted in order to terminate the contract. Automatic termination would permit a wrongdoer to choose a termination date potentially to the detriment of the wronged party.

Mr Geys' employment ended on 6 January. His actions after the employer's repudiatory breach clearly affirmed the contract. Until the bank had validly exercised its contractual right to terminate in lieu of notice — by paying the PILON and writing to him to explain their actions — his employment continued, until early January. As a result, he was entitled to the higher termination payment.

Whilst in this case it was the employer that terminated the employment, the same principles also apply to an employee. The Supreme Court confirmed that it is the employee's action (in accepting the breach and resigning) which creates the dismissal rather than the breach itself.

Malik v Bank of Credit and Commerce International [1997] IRLR 462

The 'Malik' term of mutual trust and confidence

Mr Malik and Mr Mahmud were dismissed by BCCI's liquidators on the grounds of redundancy. It subsequently came to light that BCCI had been operating fraudulently. As a result, Mr Malik and Mr Mahmud struggled to find employment. They brought a claim seeking damages, alleging that their lack of job prospects were a result of the reputational damage caused by having worked for a fraudulent company.

The House of Lords looked at various legal issues, but the relevant one here is the implied term of mutual trust and confidence. The court allowed the appeal and confirmed that the term of mutual trust and confidence would be implied by law into all employment law contracts:

"The employer must not, without reasonable and proper cause, conduct itself in a manner calculated and likely to destroy or seriously damage the relationship of trust and confidence between employer and employee."

There are two things at play here: the employer's conduct and the potential 'reasonable and proper cause' for that conduct. This case suggests that the employer's conduct must be calculated to damage the relationship of trust and confidence **and** *likely* to do so (emphasis added). However, subsequent case law has confirmed that it is an either/or test. The employer's conduct must either be calculated to destroy or seriously damage the employment relationship or be likely to do so. It doesn't have to be both.

Waltham Forest v Omilaju [2005] IRLR 35

What is capable of amounting to a 'last straw'?

Mr Omilaju brought various employment tribunal claims against the Council. They were all consolidated and dismissed in September 2001.

At all material times the Council had a policy that employees who brought employment proceedings against it are required to apply for special unpaid or annual leave to attend a tribunal hearing. My Omilaju did not do so and the Council therefore argued his absence was unauthorised and refused to pay his full salary for July and August 2001.

Mr Omilaju resigned and claimed (amongst other things) constructive dismissal, stating in his letter of resignation that the reduced pay was "*the last straw in a series of less favourable treatments that I have been subjected to over a period of years*".

The employment tribunal dismissed Mr Omilaju's constructive dismissal claim. He appealed to the EAT and subsequently to the Court of Appeal.

The Court of Appeal said that the last straw must be the last in a series of incidents which, taken together, amount to a repudiatory breach of contract. They set the following guidelines about the last straw:

- The last straw must not be completely trivial

- It doesn't have to be the same character of incident as earlier ones in the series

- The last straw doesn't have to be unreasonable or blameworthy conduct on the part of the employer by itself, although in most cases it will be

- A completely harmless act by the employer cannot be the last straw even if the employee honestly but mistakenly thinks it undermines their trust and confidence in the employer.

To expand on that slightly, Lord Dyson said:

"The question specifically raised by this appeal is: what is the necessary quality of a final straw if it is to be successfully relied on by the employee as a repudiation of the contract? […] The quality that the final straw must have is that it should be an act in a series whose cumulative effect is to amount to a breach of the implied term. I do not use the phrase "an act in a series" in a precise or technical sense. The act does not have to be of the same character as the earlier acts. Its essential quality is that, when taken in conjunction with the earlier acts on which the employee relies, it amounts to a breach of the implied term of trust and confidence. It must contribute something to that breach, although what it adds may be relatively insignificant." (para 19)

He then went on to say that:

"an entirely innocuous act on the part of the employer cannot be a final straw, even if the employee genuinely, but mistakenly, interprets the act as hurtful and destructive of his trust and confidence in his employer." (para 22)

The Court of Appeal did not agree that Mr Omilaju had been constructively dismissed. The Council's refusal to pay him for attending the tribunal, in line with its own policies, wasn't capable of being a last straw.

Kaur v Leeds Teaching Hospitals NHS Trust [2018] IRLR 833

'Can a 'last straw' incident revive a constructive dismissal claim following previously affirmed breaches? And can a fair disciplinary process ever amount to a last straw?

Ms Kaur was a nurse with Leeds Teaching Hospitals. She received a final written warning for inappropriate behaviour, which included an altercation with another member of staff. She appealed against the warning, but her appeal was dismissed.

Ms Kaur resigned and brought a claim for constructive dismissal. The 'last straw' that caused her to resign and bring a claim was the employer's dismissal of her appeal. However her claim related to a series of events over the course of several years, including the altercation with her colleague and the employer's conduct throughout disciplinary procedure. The tribunal struck out her claim for having no reasonable prospects of success. She appealed.

The issue for the Court of Appeal was whether a 'last straw' incident could allow an employee to claim constructive dismissal even when the employee had affirmed the contract following the earlier incidents that she sought to rely on. When an employee is faced with a fundamental breach of contract by an employer, he or she has the choice to either resign or stay. Once the employee has decided to stay, he or she is said to have 'affirmed' the contract and loses the right to resign and claim constructive dismissal. In Ms Kaur's case she relied on a series of incidents in the way in which she had been managed over the first two years of her employment. It was almost a year after the last of these that she was subjected to the disciplinary action that led to her final written warning. She relied on the earlier incidents as being part of the conduct that she claimed amounted to a breach of trust and confidence.

The Court of Appeal reviewed and clarified the law on 'last straws' in constructive dismissal cases:

"In the normal case where an employee claims to have been constructively dismissed it is sufficient for a tribunal to ask itself the following questions:

1. What was the most recent act (or omission) on the part of the employer which the employee says caused, or triggered, his or her resignation?

2. Has he or she affirmed the contract since that act?

3. If not, was that act (or omission) by itself a repudiatory breach of contract?

4. If not, was it nevertheless a part (applying the approach explained in Omilaju) of a course of conduct comprising several acts and omissions which, viewed cumulatively, amounted to a (repudiatory) breach of the Malik term? (If it was, there is no need for any separate consideration of a possible previous affirmation, for the reason given at the end of para. 45 above.)

5. Did the employee resign in response (or partly in response) to that breach?"

Where there is a course of conduct which cumulatively creates a repudiatory breach of contract, the last act in that series can revive earlier affirmed breaches. If Ms Kaur had accepted earlier breaches by not resigning at that point, a new breach of contract could revive them. Theoretically she could bring a constructive dismissal claim.

However, the Court of Appeal stated that a fair disciplinary process can never form part of a serious breach of contract. There was no evidence of anything improper or unfair in the employer's handling of the disciplinary proceedings. The employers conduct was not therefore capable of amounting to a 'last straw' because it could not have contributed to the undermining of the implied term of mutual trust and confidence. As a result, the appeal decision could not be a 'last straw' and the tribunal had not erred in law when striking out the case.

Buckland v Bournemouth University Higher Education Corporation University [2010] IRLR 445

Can an employer 'cure' a repudiatory breach?

Professor Buckland was a professor at Bournemouth University. One part of his role was marking examinations, which were then second-marked by a colleague to ensure consistency. The second marker endorsed the marks and the results were confirmed at a meeting of the Board of Examiners. However, after a high fail rate amongst those students who were resitting (14/16), the Chief of the Board of Examiners re-marked the papers.

Due to Mr Buckland's protestations about what had happened, the University set up an inquiry. The inquiry vindicated him, but he was dissatisfied with what he felt was an attack on his integrity as an examiner.

Mr Buckland resigned and claimed constructive dismissal. The letter of resignation was sent in February 2007, with his resignation to take effect from July 2007, i.e. the end of term. Mr Buckland deliberately gave long notice to preserve his students' academic best interests.

The EAT agreed with the tribunal that there had been a repudiatory breach, determining that the correct test for repudiatory breach of contract was an objective one. However, the EAT found that the breach had been 'cured' by the inquiry.

The Court of Appeal outlined the two main issues before them as:

"(i) Whether the conduct of an employer who is said to have committed a fundamental breach of the contract of employment is to be judged by a unitary test or a "range of reasonable responses" test.

(ii) Whether an employer who has committed a fundamental breach of contract can cure the breach while the employee is considering whether to treat it as a dismissal."

The Court of Appeal upheld the EAT's findings in relation to the correct objective test. But it disagreed with the determination that a breach can be 'cured'. Once a breach has occurred, an employer cannot 'undo' it.

The Court of Appeal made clear that there was no justification for introducing the principle into employment law that a fundamental breach, if curable and cured, removes the innocent party's option to accept.

What do you get?

1 Monthly live online 'Ask Me Anything' sessions: each month, we host an online video webinar, when you can share your HR problems and ask Daniel anything about employment law. You'll also receive a recording and a transcript each month, so you have a permanent record of the session even if you cannot be there.

"Daniel Barnett is an inspirational, walking and talking 'how to understand mind-boggling employment law handbook!"

Ellie King, HR Manager, RWE Technology

2 A specially recorded audio seminar every month, with HR shortcuts and workarounds you can't get anywhere else.

3 The monthly Inner Circular magazine, jam-packed with valuable information for ambitious HR professionals.

4 Access to Daniel's exclusive, private, invitation-only online Inner Circle group, where you get to discuss HR problems with other smart, ambitious professionals and download precedents and policies they have shared.

"It's the support and help that you get, the reassurance that you're talking to people who know what they're talking about rather than people just randomly giving information."

Nicky Jolley, HR2DAY LTD

5 Access to the exclusive HR Inner Circle website which includes a back-catalogue of all the HRIC resources since the launch in 2015.

6 After six month's membership, you become entitled to a 30 minute telephone consultation with Daniel Barnett once a year, which you can use for your most urgent and important employment law issues.

WWW.HRINNERCIRCLE.CO.UK

"This is one of the best investments in yourself and your career you will ever decide to take."

100%
Risk-Free
Guarantee

Only **£86 + VAT**
per month

No long-term contracts.
No notice periods.
No fuss.

Join today!

Also by Daniel Barnett...

EMPLOYEE INVESTIGATIONS

HOW TO CONDUCT - AND TRAIN OTHERS IN CONDUCTING - GRIEVANCE AND DISCIPLINARY INVESTIGATIONS

Book 1 in the Employment Law Library

DANIEL BARNETT

#1 on Amazon for Human Resources

GDPR
for HR
Professionals

2nd edition

Book 2 in the Employment Law Library

INCLUDED:
TEMPLATE DATA
PROTECTION POLICY
FOR EMPLOYERS,
WORKERS &
CONSULTANTS

GDPR

DANIEL BARNETT

Preventing and DEFENDING Employee STRESS CLAIMS

Book 3 in the Employment Law Library

DANIEL BARNETT

EMPLOYMENT TRIBUNAL TIME LIMITS

DANIEL BARNETT

EMPLOYMENT TRIBUNAL TIME LIMITS

Book 4 in the Employment Law Library

DANIEL BARNETT

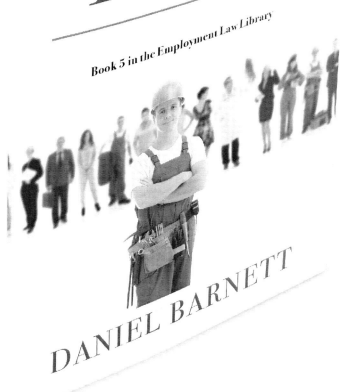

Deconstructing
TUPE

Book 5 in the Employment Law Library

DANIEL BARNETT

Changing
Terms and
Conditions

Book 6 in the Employment Law Library

DANIEL BARNETT

CHANGING TERMS AND CONDITIONS

DANIEL BARNETT

Constructive Dismissal

Book 7 in the Employment Law Library

DANIEL BARNETT

8th edition publishing October 2020

Available on Amazon

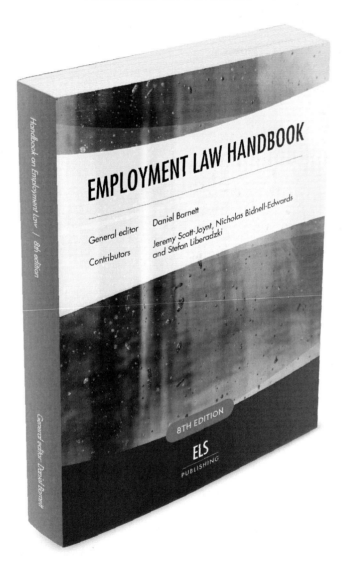

One Final Thing…

I have updated my 20 Employment Law Policies for small businesses.

If you are an HR professional, they are perfect for incorporating into a staff handbook. If you are a solicitor, they come with a licence for you to resell them or give them away for free to clients.

WWW.POLICIES2020.COM